T0128807

Reaching Our Neediest Children: Bringing a Mental Health Program Into the Schools

Reaching Our Neediest Children: Bringing a Mental Health Program Into the Schools

A Guide to Program Implementation

Jennifer Crumpley, LCSW-R
Penelope Moore, DSW, LCSW-R

TRUE DIRECTIONS
AN AFFILIATE OF TARCHER PERIGEE

iUniverse®

REACHING OUR NEEDIEST CHILDREN: BRINGING A MENTAL HEALTH PROGRAM INTO THE SCHOOLS A GUIDE TO PROGRAM IMPLEMENTATION

iUniverse books may be ordered through booksellers or by contacting:

iUniverse
1663 Liberty Drive
Bloomington, IN 47403
www.iuniverse.com
1-800-Authors (1-800-288-4677)

Because of the dynamic nature of the Internet, any web addresses or links contained in this book may have changed since publication and may no longer be valid. The views expressed in this work are solely those of the author and do not necessarily reflect the views of the publisher, and the publisher hereby disclaims any responsibility for them.

Any people depicted in stock imagery provided by Thinkstock are models, and such images are being used for illustrative purposes only.
Certain stock imagery © Thinkstock.

ISBN: 978-1-5320-0532-9 (sc)
ISBN: 978-1-5320-0531-2 (hc)
ISBN: 978-1-5320-0530-5 (e)

Library of Congress Control Number: 2016913823

Print information available on the last page.

iUniverse rev. date: 09/28/2016

Acknowledgments

Our heartfelt appreciation to those who read through our manuscript:

Cheryl A. Basch, Ed.D., for her wisdom and helpful recommendations.

Mildred Antonelli, Ph.D., for her astute observations and support.

Contents

To Patricia Leff, MD, a child psychiatrist who devoted herself to improving the emotional well-being of children, in the belief that layers of noxious social, emotional, and physical factors conspire against children and rob children of hope

Foreword

Reaching Our Neediest Children: Bringing a Mental Health Program Into the Schools

The fundamental role of public schools is to provide children with the education they need to become productive and informed members of society. Ensuring that teachers are well equipped to teach and that standards are in place for schools to be held accountable are necessary ingredients to ensure positive outcomes, but they are only part of what children require in order to learn.

Children do not come to school as blank slates, simply ready to open up to the lessons and subjects that are intended for them. From the earliest grades through high school, life experiences are always present, and many of these experiences are daunting. If our educational systems are going to succeed, the whole child must be considered.

In November 2015, the mayor of New York City released "The NYC Mental Health Roadmap," which includes data on children in public schools. As it points out, 18 % of children through age 18 experience multiple adverse events in their lives that can seriously impact well-being. The report also notes that over 25 % of all high school students experience difficult emotions, including a sense of hopelessness. While the report notes that these are factors that may predict mental illness later in life, these factors reflect the burdens that can be impediments to learning (https://thrivenyc. cityofnewyork.us/).

It makes sense to invest in mental health services in public schools. Having the capacity to address the emotional and situational issues children live with can make an enormous difference, and we have seen this benefit over the years through the work of school social workers and other mental health professionals. Their stories reflect success, time and again, across all grades.

However, mental health services will not be effective without truly thoughtful and clear understanding of public schools as the complex social systems that they are. Teachers, principals, and other school personnel have enormous responsibilities in the fast-paced, often overburdened school environment. It is imperative to bring mental health services into schools in an informed and strategic manner. To fail to do this imperils the use of critical resources.

This guidebook to the implementation of mental health services in schools, by two very experienced social work professionals, shows the way. They have developed a tool kit for mental health professionals and program administrators to follow that substantially increases the likelihood programs will take root in the school and be effective.

Many children need help, and they have a right to the best possible services. For this to work, professionals need to pay close attention to the school as a system. This guide will prove to be an essential resource for putting it all together.

Robert Schachter, DSW
Executive Director
National Association of Social Workers
New York City Chapter
December 7, 2015

Introduction

This guidebook seeks to prepare mental health professionals and related staff who wish to develop therapeutic counseling services in schools by answering this question: What does a mental health professional need to know when entering the unknown terrain of the school system to provide mental health services to children?

Goren (1996) described the process of the "school-based mental health worker entering a school for the first time as a bit like Alice as she tumbled into the Rabbit Hole and landed in the long corridor, finding it lined with locked doors" (p. 57). When considering the programmatic aspects of planning and implementing a freestanding clinic program in the schools, this conceptualization gives way to the minefield of institutional politics.

The purpose of this book is to provide tools for school-based mental health workers and other mental health professionals to use in navigating the rough terrain of this complex work. The nature of the minefield lies not only within the educational system but also in the task of effective collaboration among school, family, mental health, social service, child protective, medical, legal, religious, and all other systems that are likely to be involved with emotionally distressed children and families.

The following chapters share lessons learned from the process of planning and implementing school-based mental health programs as experienced by the authors. Through years of experience as social work professionals and directors of school-based mental health programs located in New York City, these authors have observed many children who were underserved by the mental health system. Educators and family members, as well as medical professionals, are often confused by behaviors such as bullying, fighting, withdrawal, and inattentiveness that contribute to poor school performance. There is often lack of agreement about how to support emotionally distressed youth, which compounds environmental and emotional stress for children already deprived of social, psychological, emotional, and spiritual support, as well as resources supportive of academic success.

Mental health professionals are well positioned to develop collaborative relationships between agency and school administrators in an effort to increase supportive services for vulnerable youth and their families. What better place to provide mental health services to youth than in the school setting where they spend many of their waking hours? By sharing lessons learned, the authors hope to foster a deeper appreciation for the absolute need and imperative to increase therapeutic counseling services for emotionally distressed youth.

While there is no one-size-fits-all approach, each person reading this book stands to gain practical knowledge about many dos and don'ts of planning and implementation of school-based mental health programs. The reader will also find that the information in this book can be adapted to fit a range of programs and different models of intervention. It provides practical information ranging from navigating within the school setting to assessment and intervention.

Chapters are written as stand-alone references for both mental health professionals and school personnel seeking answers to specific questions:

1. Who are our neediest children? In this chapter, a case example is used to illustrate individual and systemic issues impacting the lives of children and the unique challenges such complexities present to educators and mental health professionals in the school environment.

2. What does a mental health professional need to know about planning prior to introducing a mental health program into the public school setting? This chapter is focused on making an entry into the school and developing the foundation for a collaborative effort between the school system and the provider mental health agency.

3. What does a mental health professional need to know about the roles of relevant school personnel upon entering

the school? This chapter is focused on what is to be learned from meeting with administrators, teachers, and key personnel.

4. What does a mental health professional need to know about day-to-day program operations in order to sustain the program? This chapter is focused on the perception of stigmatization, and gaining access to the referred student.

5. What does a mental health professional need to know about the annual start-up of the new school year? This chapter is focused on what it entails to start a school-based mental health program at the beginning of each academic year.

6. What does a mental health professional need to know about identifying students who will receive program services? This chapter is focused on identifying and routing referred students to the school-based mental health worker.

7. What does a mental health professional need to know about counseling students in the program? This chapter is focused on exploring the need for mental health services, obtaining legal consent to provide therapeutic counseling services, and beginning the work with the child.

8. What does a mental health professional need to know about confidentiality and informed consent? This chapter is focused on explaining confidentiality to the child and family, and how to maintain confidentiality within the school environment.

9. What does a mental health professional need to know about individual student assessment and intervention? This chapter is focused on why the child is being referred, assessing the need, and providing mental health services in the school.

10. What does a mental health professional need to know about supervising a school-based mental health worker? This chapter is focused on the uniqueness of supervising a school-based mental health worker.

11. What does a mental health professional need to know about supervising social work, psychology, and mental health counseling interns? This chapter is focused on the fit of master-level students to the school-based mental health program.

12. What does a mental health professional need to know about staff turnover? This chapter is focused on staff turnover specific to the school-based mental health program, and how to manage it administratively.

13. What does a mental health professional need to know about summer activities? This chapter is focused on maintaining the program during summer months, when schools are operating on a summer schedule.

Finally, this book provides practical tools to effectively reach our neediest children and bring a mental health program into the schools.

Chapter 1

Who Are Our Neediest Children?

For purposes of this book, "our neediest children" are those who are most in need of therapeutic counseling services and who are the most likely to fall between the cracks within school, mental health, medical, juvenile, and social service systems. The following case vignette will provide some background as to the type of situations confronting school-age children and will illustrate how school-based mental health programs can benefit the most at-risk, vulnerable, alienated, and fragile child. It should be noted that throughout the book, "school-based mental health worker" refers to a licensed mental health professional, employed by a community-based mental health agency or hospital, and placed on-site in the school.

Case Vignette

Matthew is a 10-year-old American Black male who is in the fifth grade in a public elementary school located in a working-class neighborhood. Matthew resides with his father, mother, and 7-year-old brother in housing for low-income families. The parents' relationship, as described by the mother, is a volatile one. The mother sought help from the school guidance counselor when Matthew's behavior at home became "intolerable." The mother feels overwhelmed and angry with both of her sons because of their oppositional behavior in school. Physical punishment is used to discipline the boys.

The family was referred to the school-based mental health program, a contracted provider of clinical services via a community-based mental health agency. A licensed social worker is employed by the program in the role of a school-based mental health worker. She was assigned to work with Matthew and his parents. The school-based mental health worker's role encompasses a wide range of tasks and responsibilities. As is typical of her job assignments, the school-based mental health worker administers a biopsychosocial assessment, provides therapeutic counseling to children and family members, follows up on treatment goals and objectives, interacts with school personnel, and participates in collaborative efforts involving various school-based and community-based resource providers.

The first task for the school-based mental health worker involved conducting a thorough initial biopsychosocial assessment of Matthew and his family situation. The process began with a telephone conversation with the mother, who was invited, along with her husband, to the school-based mental health worker's school-based office. At the first meeting, the mother arrived alone; the father was unavailable to attend. The school-based mental health worker initiated an intake interview with Matthew and his mother for the purpose of completing a biopsychosocial assessment. During the intake interview, the school-based mental health worker obtained a written consent for release of information, allowing her to obtain relevant information from Matthew's teacher at a later date.

At the conclusion of the intake process, the school-based mental health worker proposed a plan to see Matthew for weekly individual therapeutic counseling sessions, and to see his mother for weekly parenting and monthly family meetings. The mother stated the father would be uninterested in attending any meetings. Interestingly, during the course of the therapeutic relationship, the mother was uncooperative and inconsistent in following through with recommendations specific to her. In fact, the mother refused to meet with the school-based mental health worker, though she was frequently seen visiting with friends in the school lobby. Regardless of the mother's absence from her scheduled sessions, the school-based mental health worker continued to see Matthew in the school for his planned weekly sessions.

During a meeting with the school-based mental health worker, Matthew's fifth-grade teacher expressed concern about his lack of respect for authority, persistent sullen demeanor, refusal to work, and conflicts with peers. Despite many attempts, the teacher had not been successful in efforts to address these problematic behaviors nor in efforts to engage the mother in problem solving.

For a few weeks after therapeutic counseling sessions began, Matthew continued to exhibit impulsive behavior. He lacked age-appropriate social skills and was prone to engage in fights. He verbalized his perception that teachers and peers "picked on" him and blamed him for various infractions of school rules. Matthew confided in the worker that he wanted to kill himself and thought of throwing himself in front of a car. He talked about beatings and burns that his mother, reportedly, had inflicted on him in the past. He asked about foster homes and group homes, because he no longer wanted to live with his parents. He told the school-based mental health worker, "No one loves me."

In light of the suicidal risk factors, the school-based mental health worker sought a psychiatric evaluation, administered by the mental health agency's staff psychiatrist. In addition, a call was made to the child protective services agency via the abuse and neglect hotline. The hotline call was made in accordance with procedures followed by mandated reporters in New York State and in collaboration with school personnel. The school-based mental health team decided, during an interdisciplinary team case conference meeting, that Matthew should continue to receive individual on-site weekly therapeutic counseling while awaiting the outcome of an investigation by the child protective services agency. In addition, communication ensued between the school-based mental health worker, staff psychiatrist, mental health agency director, teacher, guidance counselor, and principal about Matthew's school-based needs, which resulted in fewer punitive measures by the teacher within the classroom.

The psychiatric evaluation determined that Matthew was not at suicidal risk. As a result of the call to the child protective services hotline, the mother received parenting skills training and supportive services. The father did not make himself available at any time. Matthew continued to receive individual weekly therapeutic counseling within the school setting.

Though Matthew's mother did not engage in recommended school-based therapeutic counseling sessions, she ceased undermining Matthew's involvement in counseling, as she had in the past. Within a few months, Matthew's behavior changed. There was a decrease in impulsivity and fighting. He experienced improved relationships with peers. There were no reports of violence in the home. Matthew's confidence grew as he developed new coping strategies and problem solving skills. His teachers no longer complained of oppositional and disrespectful behavior.

To understand the school-based mental health worker's effective intervention in this case, it is necessary to understand the sociocultural context of Matthew's life, and to apply social systems theory and an ecological perspective. Social systems theory presents an analytical approach emphasizing the interrelatedness and mutual interdependence of systems, which highlights the multi-causal context of human behavior (Greene & Frankel, 1994).

When applied to individual, family, and group and community functioning, it provides a conceptual framework that explains and increases understanding about the complex interactions among various systems in Matthew's life, such as his family, school, and the larger community.

Similarly, application of ecological theory sheds light on the quality of social supports, the size of the support network, and the relative degrees of stress associated with each aspect of Matthew's interpersonal relationships. Consequently, strategies of intervention can be arranged in such a way as to mitigate stressful interactions and maximize client strengths and resources. A blend of direct client and environmental actions aimed at restructuring resources helps to make for a better adaptive fit between the individual client system(s) and the larger environment (Lewis & Greene, 1994).

Matthew's acting-out behavior, leading to academic failure, came to be understood within the context of interactions between social and environmental factors that interfered with his school performance. The vignette illustrates how the teacher was able to expedite communication quickly due to the proximity of the school-based mental health worker, given that they worked in the same building. The teacher and key school personnel frequently contacted the school-based mental health worker regarding Matthew's needs, fostering the teacher's reliance on the school-based mental health worker for support and consultation. In return, the school-based mental health worker reached out to school personnel as needed. The teacher and pupil personnel team

(PPT) had ongoing interactions with the school-based mental health worker via phone calls and meetings. Thus, communication was enhanced in managing crises that emerged during the course of therapeutic counseling. If the school-based mental health worker had not been located within the school, it is questionable if the teacher would have given the time and effort to contacting an outside resource or would have even known whom to contact.

Teachers frequently attempt to manage problematic behaviors within the classroom in idiosyncratic ways. However, in this case scenario, the teacher had been introduced to the school-based mental health worker during an orientation session in which teachers throughout the school setting were apprised of the services offered by the school-based mental health program. As a result, the teacher gained information that made her aware she would not be left alone with the personal information she was hearing from Matthew. Furthermore, being on-site in the school, the school-based mental health worker obtained more reliable information about Matthew's behavior through direct observation of the child in various contexts within the school—hallways, lunchroom, classroom—as well as from anecdotal reports given by school personnel.

The school-based mental health worker's presence had meaning for Matthew. He was able to see her and wave to her in the hallway. This positively affected his progress, especially when therapy was suspended for a month when Matthew's mother denied permission for him to attend sessions. The school-based mental health worker's visibility within the school diminished

Matthew's feelings of abandonment and enhanced his belief that the school-based mental health worker would be there for him.

The school's PPT and the entire school-based mental health team cooperated in developing an appropriate treatment plan. This highlights the fact that the school-based mental health worker is not an island unto herself. The school-based mental health worker is expected to work closely and share information appropriately with the PPT and attend regularly scheduled PPT meetings. Consequently, school personnel were sensitized to Matthew's emotional needs and exercised increased caution in their communication with his mother so as not to trigger or exacerbate conflicts in the parent-child relationship. For example, careful attention was given to the wording of notes sent home, to minimize the risk of future incidences of physical punishment.

Not only did the school's PPT work collaboratively with the school-based mental health worker and mental health team to help the family, but the school-based mental health worker vigorously called upon her own clinical expertise, communication skills, and stamina to best help Matthew.

The Need

Current Population Survey Supplement data (1999) report that 18 % of all school-age children (ages 5–17) experience multiple risk factors associated with poor academic performance. The fact that the level of multiple risk exposure is as great for young children as it is for older children represents a serious issue for child well-being and school adjustment (Kominski, Jamieson, & Martinez, 2001). Research studies (Cantor, Smolover, & Stamler, 2010; Walker & Smithgall, 2009; Cusick, Goerge, & Bell, 2009; Dworsky, 2008; Mayer, 2005; and Yang & Goerge, 2005) also document a relationship between a high concentration of at-risk youth and a school being identified as underperforming, because when children who are encountering multiple factors that place them "at risk" interact in the same academic environment with those who do not carry this label, it becomes difficult, if not impossible, for teachers to teach and students to learn. In these authors' experiences, it takes only one child to disrupt an entire classroom, detracting a teacher's time and attention from the class as a whole.

Some factors that place youth at risk are listed below:

- Depression
- Anger
- Physical abuse
- Sexual abuse
- Emotional neglect
- Bullying
- Loss and bereavement
- Peer pressure
- Family problems

- Poverty
- Homelessness
- Anxiety
- School-related stress
- Chronic illness
- Somatic complaints
- Foster care placements
- Gangs
- Sexual acting-out
- Impaired language skills
- Developmental disabilities
- Poor academic performance
- Domestic violence
- Alcohol and/or substance abuse
- Social media
- Involvement with child welfare and other social service systems

The literature suggests that interventions designed to overcome barriers to successfully launching and sustaining supportive services within schools are best guided by cross-systems approaches. As in the case of Matthew, adapting an ecological systems perspective can also be particularly helpful in the process of thinking through the planning and implementation phases of developing a school-based mental health program. The ecological perspective enables the mental health worker to evaluate what perceptions are operating, what gaps exist, and what adaptations/ modifications are needed to align the mission and goals of such a program within the host setting. Misalignment could result in conflicts between mental health professionals, school administrators, teachers, pupil personnel, and support staff, as well as threaten program survival.

Awareness of the perils and pitfalls of forging linkages in the service of children and their families is crucial. Overcoming barriers to developing school-based mental health programs involves educational bureaucracies, mental health providers, and funding sources successfully negotiating a contract that will directly benefit children in dire need of therapeutic services. Without the coordinated effort and hard work of all, and despite good intentions, programs will falter as a result of misunderstanding and a lack of focus on the best interests of children.

One might conclude that the educational system would welcome the help of mental health professionals as an additional resource. However, several obstacles may stand in the way of schools welcoming "outside" mental health professionals.

The following is a list of potential areas of conflict that may make entry into the schools difficult:

- The school system may view outside mental health professionals as siphoning away jobs from school personnel.
- Teachers and administrators may be confused about mental health services and may lack understanding about what mental health services have to offer.

- Teachers and administrators may feel that involving an outside agency will mean additional work for them.
- School personnel may view the school-based mental health worker as having a less stressful work environment (e.g., having privileges, working in a comfortable environment, and having fewer children to work with).

The remainder of this book provides a step-by-step approach to successfully launching a school-based mental health program, which is built on the core principles of compromise, sharing resources, open communication, ongoing dialogue, and mutual respect for all professionals in their respective roles of serving our neediest children.

Chapter 2

What Does a Mental Health Professional Need to Know About Planning Prior to Introducing a Mental Health Program Into the Public School Setting?

Planning Phase

B ringing a new project into the educational system takes careful planning and a well-thought-out strategy, culminating in a formal contract with the host school. In order to gain entry, one must market the uniqueness of the school-based mental health program's mission in relation to the environmental context in which it hopes to thrive and conduct business.

The initial phase of program development involves the process of tuning in to the political context of the school and allied partners, such as the district superintendent, director of pupil personnel teams, director of student support services, director of special education, and director of special programs. (Titles may differ from region to region.) The development of positive working relationships with power brokers within the educational system sets the stage for planning and successful program implementation.

Depending on state and city governments, there will be different affiliates joining to offer school-based mental health program services. For example, a New York City program generally includes a large agency, such as a hospital or community-based mental health agency, that has entered into an agreement with the New York City Department of Education to provide services to a particular target population within a designated school.

Initial conversations can potentially make or break the program, depending on the communication process and based on the individual agendas of the participants. For example, school personnel may be threatened by an outsider coming into the school. They may perceive that a new program will heap more work on them. There may be some resentment if an office is taken away from existing school personnel to accommodate the school-based mental health worker. Newly hired school administrators may be reluctant to bring a program into the school until they know the lay of the land. These are just a few of the reasons one must bring clarity to the work of school-based mental health services and explain how the school-based mental health worker will function and interact within the school system, to the benefit of all.

Ideally, there will be a second phase to program development. This will include a meeting with the principals plus leaders of the various agencies that provide other school-based student support services. The purpose of this meeting is to share a common vision about what needs to be done, by whom, and how. This entails an open exchange about the vision for the school-based mental health program and the mission. Knowing one's mission predetermines who the client will be. For example, if the mission is prevention of substance abuse, prevention of placement in special education, or decreasing school violence, then these narrowly defined parameters will guide one's thinking about the target population to be served and the selection process for identifying students to be served.

In addition to reviewing the vision and mission, the partners will explore the areas where there may be duplication of services. What the authors have learned from prior experience is that the school population is made up of different categories of youth at risk "for something." Therefore, a school-based mental health program has to be careful not to duplicate or threaten existing programs or student support service providers based within the school or within the larger community. This second-phase conversation will help to map existing school-based support services and will minimize the risk for duplication of services.

Reaching agreement about the most effective, efficient mechanism for working and communicating with one another is an essential aspect of building and sustaining trust in relationships among key players, as is recognizing that each partner may be unfamiliar with the organizational culture, procedures, and protocols of the other. Once the questions of who does what, with whom, and how have been agreed upon, the foundation is laid to formally contract to provide mental health services within the designated school.

Do not be fooled into thinking that laying the groundwork for a formal contract is the same as saying that everyone is in agreement about the placement of services. Resistance can be virulent at the local level.

Arguments against a school-based mental health program often find their origins in political and territorial matters. It may mean that the school must give up precious space typically used for academics to a nonacademic program. School personnel may think there will be more work created for them by the addition of this support service.

On the flip side of the coin, school personnel may view the program as taking work away from them. Some resistance may be due to simple jealousy. For example, the quality and attractiveness of office furnishings and equipment supplied by an agency for a school-based mental health worker may outshine those of a school employee. Therefore, anticipate resistance and delay to the start of the program when there is a lack of understanding about the program's services and when outstanding issues remain unresolved.

Lastly, it is advantageous for the provider mental health agency to establish a central office away from the school, to be used as a home base. This office can be used for meetings and for storing case records and other documents. Though meetings with school personnel, children, and family members usually take place in the school setting, meetings can also take place at the central office, in the evenings, and whenever school is closed or as necessary. The added advantage of a central office is that the school-based mental health worker can be away from the fishbowl of the school.

To minimize the risk of a delay in the process in introducing the school-based mental health program to a school, the authors propose an orientation and planning for collaboration. (See Appendix I.)

Helpful Hints

- Tune in to the political context of the school and allied partners.
- Strive for transparency in communication.
- Clarify vision, mission, and goals of the school-based mental health program.
- Avoid duplication of services.
- Reach for agreement between the school and the mental health agency each step of the way.
- Set up a central office.

Chapter 3

What Does a Mental Health Professional Need to Know About the Roles of Relevant School Personnel Upon Entering the School?

Getting Started

- Determine which schools will receive school-based mental health services.
- Secure a formal agreement between partners.
- Ensure that partners understand the services to be offered.
- Clarify roles and responsibilities of the school-based mental health worker.
- Review the potential impact on children to be served.
- Identify funding sources.
- Confirm the start date for the school-based mental health program.

The mental health provider (hospital or community-based mental health agency) has the responsibility of thinking through many of the necessary details regarding the best way and in what manner to introduce the concept of bringing mental health services to the schools. For example, if services are to be provided in more than one school within a school district, a joint meeting with principals, representatives from the school district, and relevant school personnel is recommended prior to services being introduced.

A formal agreement must be secured between the partners, detailing the scope of mental health services to be provided on-site in the school. To prepare for this agreement and to avoid obstacles to the success of a newly established school-based mental health program, the authors recommend a meeting with key school administrators (e.g., principals and assistant principals) to introduce the program and to verify what the administrators know or do not know about the school-based mental health program.

Assume the administrators have *not* been given the details of the programs by the school district. Assume the administrators do *not* understand the concept of school-based mental health services, even when they have already been given an orientation. Last but not least, assume the administrators are *not* in agreement that a school-based mental health program should be placed in their schools. Expect the unexpected in your first meeting with school administrators.

Whenever possible, prior to a meeting, distribute written materials electronically. These materials may include a program plan, fact sheets, program start date, months of operation, days and hours of operation, target population to be served, number of children to be served, and size of caseloads to be assumed by the school-based mental health worker. At the meeting, a minimal amount of hard copy materials may be distributed, including brochures. These materials might also include program information, statistical data, and performance outcomes. Together, these materials describe what the provider mental health agency has to offer.

Define the target population. Clear communication is critical when identifying the population to be served, the type of intervention, and the scope of services, including any limitations posed by funding and regulatory restrictions. Be prepared, knowing that school personnel may not readily understand or accept the parameters within which school-based mental services will be provided.

Describe the staffing pattern, size, and qualifications of the school-based mental health team members. Review tasks and responsibilities of the assigned school-based mental health worker and the reporting structure. This is key to forging a positive relationship with school personnel, by defining roles and boundaries and dispelling myths about extra work school personnel may think they will be given. A clear articulation of the school-based mental health worker's job description, and agreement between both parties regarding same, can minimize the risk of any misunderstanding about what the school-based mental health worker is expected to do and to whom the worker is expected to report.

The school-based mental health worker should be viewed as the expert regarding the child's mental health needs as opposed to a program director, supervisor, or other administrator not directly involved in providing therapeutic counseling. However, accountability rests with the mental health provider agency to supervise and administer all aspects of the school-based mental health program.

Discuss the potential for possibly stigmatizing children who receive school-based mental health services. Often school personnel have many questions about the possibility of children being stigmatized. The meeting is an opportunity to answer questions, give feedback, educate school staff, explain the partnership between the mental health service provider and the school, and demonstrate how it will serve the best interests of children in need of on-site mental health services.

School-based mental health programs are affiliated with agencies that have policies and procedures that do not mimic those of the local or state department of education (DOE). It is crucial that the mental health agency and school system recognize and respect the other's mission, philosophy, and goals. An important first step to achieving this goal is for the school-based mental health worker to obtain the DOE's most recent policies and procedures manual and to become familiar with relevant information.

Clarify who will fund these services. Some school-based mental health programs are paid for by grant funds, whereas others will accept Medicaid or other health insurances. Mental health agencies and the DOE must come to an agreement about payments for services. A program's duration and sustainability are dependent on the nature of the funding. Where there is an agreement regarding payment for services vis-à-vis client referrals, the liaison who routes the referrals must explore the family's ability to pay for services. This is for the purpose of ensuring the financial viability of the program. Of note: governmental regulatory bodies often require that the child be given a diagnosis as defined by the *Diagnostic and Statistical Manual of Mental Disorders* (DSM) or by the *International Classification of Diseases* (ICD).

School administrators must designate a liaison to the school-based mental health program. The guidance counselor is a good choice for this role. It will be beneficial to the collaboration for the liaison to be objective and to value school-based mental health services. Classroom teachers should not fill this role, given the need for confidentiality about a student's life situation.

Helpful Hints

- Meet with key school administrators to provide an orientation about the school-based mental health program's mission, goals, and services.
- Prior to the orientation, disseminate written materials electronically, when possible. Distribute a minimal amount of hard copy written materials.

- Define the purpose of the partnership between the school and the agency's school-based mental health team.
- Describe the responsibilities and tasks of the school-based mental health worker.
- Clarify roles and boundaries as they relate to school personnel vs. the school-based mental health worker.
- Expect the unexpected.

Entering the School

Gaining entry into the school must be undertaken with awareness and sensitivity to multiple factors.

Plan and conduct an introductory meeting at the beginning of the school year. Ideally, this is an in-auditorium forum for teachers and school personnel. Introduce the key mental health agency professionals, answer questions, hand out brochures and business cards, and distribute fliers with factual information about the program. It's best for fliers to be printed on colored paper that will not easily get lost on teachers' desks. Fliers should include names, titles, and contact information of all key mental health personnel, especially the designated go-to troubleshooter for the school-based mental health program.

The school-based mental health worker must be introduced to relevant school personnel. Some introductions can be made on an individual basis. Others can take place in a group format (e.g., during the first school meeting of the year). These introductions should include administrators, guidance staff, psychologists, teachers, parent advocates, clerical assistants, front-desk personnel, safety and security officers, cafeteria staff, maintenance staff, and others.

Extremely important is an introduction to the school's clerical staff: those involved with the routine business of school life, such as greeting families, receiving and distributing mail, answering telephone calls, responding to general inquiries, directing deliveries, and so on. The initial meeting with clerical staff is an opportunity to provide the school-based mental health worker with an organizational chart and information about school policies and procedures, such as bell schedules, disciplinary procedures, emergency response protocols, school calendar, academic curricula, location of in-school mailboxes, access to restrooms and lounges, parking information, office keys, and much more. Making friends with front-desk personnel can facilitate situations such as gaining access to a copy machine, obtaining a bathroom key, or being notified of a delivery.

Private office space is required for the school-based mental health worker in order to ensure confidentiality. Unfortunately, the reality is that privacy is not easily accomplished in overcrowded urban settings. School-based mental health programs are often asked to share space, during the same hours, with another provider. This type of arrangement is unacceptable and inappropriate for the purposes of therapeutic counseling. A large classroom filled with chairs and distracting stimuli, such as computers, is similarly not suitable for individual and group therapeutic counseling, due to the size and setup of the room.

The mental health supervisor/director must be a staunch advocate for the school-based mental health program's need for appropriate space. This requires firsthand inspection by the supervisor. The supervisor must take a look at the office space before occupancy. This should be done every year.

Also, a decision has to be made as to who is responsible for the provision of and payment for business necessities such as a phone line, cell phones, computers, Internet access, furniture, copy machine, file and storage cabinets, and other equipment. Does the school or mental health agency provide these items? What is needed, and who will pay for what?

It is necessary to determine how children will be identified or referred to the program within the school. What will be the process? No matter who makes the referrals, the teacher must be made fully aware of the process because the teacher will be responsible for allowing the child to leave the room to attend the therapy session.

Classroom teachers are instrumental in the process of identification because they are in the best position to observe a child's maladaptive behavior and to report on it. For example, teachers can be taught to use behavioral checklists and to review the results in discussion with the school-based mental health worker, for the purposes of problem solving and treatment planning. Teachers are the ones most likely to request therapy and supportive therapeutic counseling for the child, especially when the child is constantly disruptive in the classroom.

A liaison, usually the guidance counselor, should be designated for the purpose of routing referrals to the school-based mental health worker. This liaison is identified by the school system. There should be a standardized procedure for referring children to the program. Using one person for routing the referrals helps to avoid confusion and allows for the educational system to keep track of a child's active or inactive status within the school-based mental health program.

The person who routes referrals to the program has the responsibility to forward the necessary information to the school-based mental health worker. The liaison obtains the identities of children in need of mental health services, and coordinates services between the school-based mental health program and other school-based support services for at-risk children.

A determination has to be made, in collaboration with school personnel, as to the time of day the child will receive mental health services. These services take various forms—for example, individual, family, and/or group therapy; recreational and cultural activities; supportive therapeutic counseling; mentoring; afterschool groups; and more. Determining when children are to be involved with the school-based mental health program during the course of the school day is at the discretion of the principal, in accordance with educational policies defining when a child can be released from class for nonacademic activities.

The school-based mental health program's hours of operation must be established. These hours are determined by such things as funding, policies and procedures of the provider mental health agency, school calendar, assessment of the unique needs of targeted populations within school, hours that school buildings are open, availability of space at the school and at the provider agency, and professional and personal leave time of individual mental health professionals assigned to a particular school setting.

The provider mental health agency must determine how the school-based mental health worker will function when a school is closed for half days, holidays, and summer months. Typically, school-based mental health services are best provided during the academic year. Due to events such as mandatory summer school for some children, coupled with the closings of some school buildings, mental health staff must plan creatively to maintain contact with children during the summer months. Most provider mental health agencies offer therapeutic counseling services to the school-based population at their central office, or strive to provide school-based therapeutic group experiences for students who seek services during the summer months.

Summer group activities frequently take the form of recreational and cultural activities hosted by a school. The summer host school may differ from the school where mental health services are provided during the academic year.

Helpful Hints

- Plan and conduct an introductory meeting at the beginning of the school year.
- Introduce the school-based mental health worker to relevant school personnel.
- Designate a school liaison.
- Establish the referral process.
- Secure private office space, appropriate to the needs of the population to be served.
- Decide who is to equip the private office space.
- Determine hours of program operation throughout the year, including summer months.

Chapter 4

What Does a Mental Health Professional Need to Know About Day-to-Day Program Operations in Order to Sustain the Program?

Program in Operation

Now that the program is ready to get up and running, there are some practical matters to address. One is getting the child out of the classroom in order to provide therapeutic counseling, which leads to the question of stigmatization.

Professionals and families have asked the question, "Won't children feel stigmatized and labeled for receiving mental health services in the school?" From our observation and anecdotally speaking, children have reported they are made to feel special when given the attention of the school-based mental health worker. That is to say, they appreciate a professional who provides a safe place for them to be heard and to voice their feelings, whether verbally or through play, whether in an individual meeting or in a group.

In fact, it is not unusual for a classmate to ask to go with their fellow student when the referred child is released from class to see a school-based mental health worker. Some students, in group therapy, have voiced pride in being in a "special club." Others enjoy having their own individual counselor. Frequently, students will seek out the school-based mental health worker between scheduled appointments. It is true that this seeking may be an excuse to get out of class, but often it is for a perceived, immediate need. This happens, for the most part, when the child is suffering from anxiety. Children are not thinking of labels when they are in distress.

To decrease the risk of stigmatization, the authors recommend the following:

- Eliminate the words "mental health" from the school-based mental health program's name. Decide upon a neutral sounding name (e.g., Winning Stars).
- Any identifying signs or correspondence should minimize or eliminate the use of "mental health."
- Use wording such as "supportive counseling" or other nontoxic vocabulary when writing to or speaking with parents about services being offered.
- Explain mental health to parents in terms of mental wellness. Make clear that the child is not "crazy."

The school-based mental health worker must learn to navigate within the culture of the school environment. For example, teachers expect to be given information about the child's progress and are known to informally request updates about the student's therapeutic progress. However, the Health Insurance Portability and Accountability Act (HIPAA) laws and state mental health regulations require confidentiality. There is usually one-way confidentiality between the school-based mental health worker and school personnel. This means that the school personnel can typically share information about the child, but the school-based mental health worker cannot give information without a signed consent for release of information.

The school-based mental health worker is advised to learn and abide by a host of educational policies and procedures. These include planning appointments for the school-based counseling sessions within the context of educational rules and regulations.

It is extremely important to negotiate a schedule with the teacher for the child's release from the classroom. Clarify when the child can miss a class on a regular basis without there being a detrimental effect on the child's academic performance. If the child does miss a class regularly, how will schoolwork be made up? Getting a child released from the class involves negotiating with the teacher about which class the child will be excused from, the time of day the child will be released, how much time will be spent in each counseling session, and the frequency of sessions during the school week. It is best to set regularly scheduled appointment times. Ensure that counseling session start and end times are clearly understood and agreed upon by the teacher, student, and legal guardian.

Determine if the child is allowed to travel alone when going to and from the school-based mental health office. At what age and under what circumstances can the child travel without an escort? The child is not to use the program as an excuse to get out of class or roam the hallways.

If an unescorted child does not show up to the school-based program office within a reasonable time frame, the school-based mental health worker must explore the circumstances. Maybe the child is absent due to illness or is on a class trip. The reason for an absence must be investigated.

Helpful Hints

- Create a neutral-sounding name for the program without using the words "mental health."
- Maintain confidentiality when responding to requests for information about the student's progress in therapeutic counseling.
- Set regularly scheduled appointment times.
- Learn and abide by educational policies and procedures with regard to scheduling counseling session appointments.
- When a child misses a scheduled appointment, investigate the reason.

Chapter 5

What Does a Mental Health Professional Need to Know About the Annual Start-Up of the New School Year?

Annual Start-Up

The planning phase for the successful start-up of the school-based mental health program and entry into the school setting requires a dialogue with school personnel during the summer months, if not sooner, to confirm plans for the start-up of the program. This is essential whether the program is new to the school or continuing from the preceding year. This dialogue is used to confirm the start date of the program, the availability of the school-based mental health program office space, the hours of operation of the program, the assignment of a designated liaison, the exchange of pertinent contact information, and the process by which the program will be rolled out within the school. A presentation to school faculty by the school-based mental health worker at the beginning of each school year is effective. An annual presentation reminds teachers of the program's existence and introduces the program to new teachers.

Introductions should be made between the school-based mental health worker and the designated school liaison. This is an opportune time to arrange for participation in various ongoing student support services meetings—for example, pupil personnel team (PPT), student support team, or other student intervention teams. The school-based mental health worker and appropriate school personnel should exchange contact information both for work and emergency situations.

The school-based mental health worker is advised to complete various tasks before the first day of operations to aid in the smooth flow of the program, thus enabling children to receive services in an appropriate and timely manner. These tasks include obtaining office supplies, equipment, and therapeutic counseling and play materials. The school-based mental health program supervisor should inspect the location, size, and cleanliness of the school-based office.

All office equipment must be available and intact, including desk, chair, outside telephone line, cell phone, printer, copier, file cabinets, paper supplies, and other necessary supplies. The office should be clean, attractively decorated, and welcoming.

If possible, an office will be equipped with such items as a desktop copier, mini refrigerator, and microwave oven in order to maximize worker efficiency. It is not unusual to have restricted use of a school's copy machine. However, having immediate access to one's own copier is essential for such things as copying a medical insurance card for billing purposes, or report cards and correspondence to be filed in the case record.

The office is to be available for use solely by the school-based mental health worker during the designated operating hours of the school-based mental health program. If the office is shared space, it is to be used by school personnel at times other than the scheduled school-based mental health program hours.

Helpful Hints

- Begin a dialogue with school personnel during the summer months to prepare for entry into the school after the summer.
- Introduce the school-based mental health worker to relevant school personnel.
- Arrange for the school-based mental health worker to participate in various ongoing student support services meetings.
- Ensure that the office space is available, equipped, clean, decorated, and welcoming.
- Confirm that the office space is not being used by other school personnel during the hours of operation set aside for the school-based mental health program.

Chapter 6

What Does a Mental Health Professional Need to Know About Identifying Students Who Will Receive Program Services?

Identification of Students

A designated school liaison is key to finding your client niche. This person will route, track, and monitor referrals to the program, act as a troubleshooter, and assist with problem solving between the mental health service provider and the school.

The principal or the assistant principal may designate the school liaison, or the designation may happen via a team structure. For example, the PPT may assume responsibility for designating the school liaison. Frequently, a designated school liaison is part of the school-based support team of the school. A classroom teacher should not be a designated liaison because of confidentiality.

Great care is required in identifying an appropriate school liaison, particularly if school personnel are not clear about the goals of the program. It is important to consider someone who can be objective, who understands how children will benefit by receiving services, and who values the contributions a school-based mental health program offers.

The authors' experiences suggest that assistant principals and guidance counselors tend to be the best liaisons. They make the most appropriate referrals because of their availability to the critical mass of students. They obtain more reliable information about students' performances both inside and outside the classroom.

In reality, once a program becomes established, referrals flow from a variety of sources. However, to minimize confusion and mixed signals, it is best to establish a standardized procedure. Make and route referrals via the school liaison for consistency and accountability purposes. The referral process should be agreed upon between the school and mental health agency.

Sometimes, referrals are not appropriate for the program. For example, if a child with special needs is receiving individual or group therapy provided by a school social worker as part of his individualized educational plan (IEP), he or she will likely not be considered an appropriate referral for the school-based mental health program due to duplication of services. Likewise, if a child is receiving mental health counseling outside of the school setting, additional in-school mental health counseling services would be inappropriate and burdensome for the child and family.

Helpful Hints

- Designate a school liaison to act as a go-between for the school system and mental health agency.
- Referrals are routed, tracked, and monitored by the liaison.
- Do not use a classroom teacher as the liaison.
- Maintain a standardized referral procedure in accordance with the agreement established between the school and the mental health agency.
- Determine if a referral is appropriate for the program.

Chapter 7

What Does a Mental Health Professional Need to Know About Counseling Students in the Program?

Counseling the Student

Policies and procedures of the school-based mental health program are, ideally, written in a manual and distributed to all school-based mental health staff. Information appropriate for the manual may include, but is not limited to, orientation guidelines, setting up office space, obtaining consent for treatment, educational policies and procedures, confidentiality instructions, school personnel contact information, school-based mental health team members' contact information, procedures for crisis intervention, and procedures for contacting child protective services and other emergency services.

Beginning therapeutic counseling involves obtaining consent for treatment. First and foremost for the purposes of obtaining consent, it is necessary to verify the child's legal guardian. Is the legal guardian a biological parent? A relative? A custodial agency? Legal guardians and caregivers may or may not be the same person. Therefore, it is essential that the school-based mental health worker learn who is authorized to provide consent for treatment. In some states, it is legal for a minor to sign consent for treatment if contacting a parent poses a threat to the child's safety or well-being. In the case of an out-of-home placement, the consent might be signed by a representative of a child protective services agency or foster care agency.

For the purpose of simplification, the child's legal guardian will be referred to as the "parent" in this and future sections of this book.

The parent should be contacted prior to meeting with and engaging the child. It is recommended that the initial contact be made by the designated school liaison. The liaison is in the best position to describe to the parent the reason for referring the student for therapeutic counseling. Thus, when the mental health worker contacts the parent to set up an appointment for the first meeting, it will not be a surprise to the parent. Connecting with parents requires obtaining pertinent information—for example, the parents' names and telephone numbers, which are usually filed in the school's main office.

The purpose of the first meeting is to explore the reason the child was referred to the program. During this meeting, the school-based mental health worker makes an introduction, explains the mission of the school-based mental health program, describes the services to be provided, and explains the manner in which they are provided (e.g., individual, group, and/or family therapy). The mental health worker explains how and why the school referred the child for therapeutic counseling and inquires as to the parent's perception of what the child needs help with. Establishing a "contract" for services with the child and parent includes discussing the plan for treatment, explaining expectations regarding attendance, and answering all questions and concerns the child may have about receiving mental health services in the school. It is necessary to explain confidentiality, how this is maintained, and under what circumstances it is *not* maintained.

At the time of this meeting, the school-based mental health worker will obtain written consent for treatment and consents for release of information from medical and other health and mental health providers currently or previously used by the child. If consent for treatment is not obtained immediately, it places the therapeutic process at risk for being terminated. Therapy cannot be provided without consent.

Engaging the child in treatment requires a broad-based assessment of the problem and planning for services consistent with the child's needs as well as with the mission of the agency. Beginning the work is also contingent upon other factors pertaining to the broader program's mission, which is generally influenced by the culture, philosophy, and orientation of the agency. For example, programs focused on prevention of out-of-home placement might engage the child, family, and other adults in different ways than those programs that provide traditional therapeutic treatment modalities. There is no one way to begin the work after the practical matters are taken care of. Nonetheless, a biopsychosocial assessment is necessary. Thus, it is best to use a standardized assessment tool when gathering information.

Explore if the child is receiving other mental health or supportive counseling services inside or outside of school. Determine how you will collaborate with other school-based support services and/ or outside providers so as not to duplicate services. Last but not least, speak with the child's teacher at the first opportunity, to obtain information about the child's overall functioning in the classroom.

Helpful Hints

- Identify the legal guardian for the purpose of obtaining a written consent for treatment.
- Explore the referral problems with the child and parent.
- Obtain written consents for release of information from varied health providers.
- Use a standardized protocol for completing a biopsychosocial assessment.
- Obtain information about the child's overall functioning in the classroom.

Chapter 8

What Does a Mental Health Professional Need to Know About Confidentiality and Informed Consent?

Confidentiality and Informed Consent

What does *confidentiality* mean? It depends on who you are speaking to and under what circumstances.

Let's begin with your first meeting with the referred student. One of the most important steps in establishing trust between the student and mental health worker is to ensure that the child understands that whatever is discussed will not be shared with others without that child's permission. In a relationship based upon confidentiality, one is not allowed to share any information discussed between the school-based mental health worker and the child without the child's and/or parent's signed consent. However, there are at least two exceptions.

First, if a child is at risk for suicide, then the worker must "betray" confidentiality. Suicidal ideation or attempts will be brought to the attention of the appropriate caregivers, school administrators, and, if necessary, medical personnel. This aspect of confidentiality (i.e., there is no confidentiality in the context of suicidal ideation) is told to the child during the first meeting between the child and mental health worker. Notably, when the child expresses the desire to seriously injure, hurt, or kill him- or herself, or when the child has made an attempt to seriously injure or kill him- or herself, these behaviors warrant the immediate attention of social service and medical support systems in order to alleviate the child's emotional distress.

Second, if a child expresses the desire to seriously injure or kill someone else, then the worker must "betray" confidentiality. Under these circumstances, the child has expressed the desire or has attempted to kill.

It is not only when a child is at suicidal or homicidal risk that one would inform other significant adults. Information should also be communicated if a child is involved in self-injurious behaviors, especially where firearms may be involved. Self-injurious behaviors include self-cutting, jumping from one rooftop to another, riding on the outside of a bus by hanging on to the rear, purposefully running into the street in the path of oncoming cars, and other activities of this nature. The child may not have verbally expressed suicidal ideation or intent. However, these types of activities put the student at great risk for personal injury, and are activities about which his or her caregivers and social support systems should be made aware.

Thus, it is crucial at the outset to educate the student about the nature of confidentiality so there is no mistaking what the expectations are when the child meets with the school-based mental health worker on an ongoing basis. The student needs to experience the mental health office as a safe space where the student will not be judged or unduly criticized by the mental health worker. Interestingly enough, when a young person reports troubling thoughts and behaviors, it is usually a cry for help that cannot be ignored. It is the mental health worker's responsibility to work toward securing the resources needed to afford the child relief.

It is true that in many situations, the student may initially balk at the notion of other people knowing about her or his innermost thoughts and feelings. This may be expressed as anger toward the worker. In the long term, however, such children will get the attention they need to address issues of concern.

Another aspect of confidentiality pertains to how much one tells school personnel. School personnel are informed at the outset about how much information can be appropriately shared without a signed consent for release of information. Being school-based means that one is, essentially, working in a fishbowl. Teachers, guidance staff, and administrators soon come to learn which children are receiving services. It is not long before school staff may ask for a report on the child's progress or ask questions about the child's functioning.

This is often a sincere attempt by school personnel to learn more about the child in order to better understand why the child behaves in a particular manner. Unfortunately, this type of questioning can put a school-based mental health worker in an awkward position. The worker cannot answer questions about the child's functioning without first receiving informed and written consent from the child's parent.

Another related issue is making a report to the appropriate child protective services regarding allegations of child abuse and neglect. As mandated reporters, mental health workers are required to report child abuse and/or neglect to the appropriate child protective services agency or hotline, in accordance with the law. Ideally, making a report is a collaborative effort between the school-based mental health worker and school personnel, depending upon who is the recipient of the allegations of abuse.

For example, when an allegation of physical or sexual abuse is made by a child to the school-based mental health worker, it is expected that the worker will inform the designated school staff. Consequently, a joint report is to be made by school personnel and the mental health worker to child protective services. This results in a collaborative effort toward establishing a safeguard for the child's emotional and physical well-being.

Helpful Hints

- Explain confidentiality to the student, family, and school personnel, and under what circumstances the school-based mental health worker must "betray" confidentiality.
- Maintain confidentiality when questioned by school personnel about the child's functioning.
- Determine the process between the school and the mental health agency for making a report to child protective services, as required by law for mandated reporters.

Chapter 9

*What Does a Mental Health
Professional Need to Know About
Assessment and Intervention?*

Assessment and Intervention

What does the child understand about why he or she is being referred for school-based therapeutic counseling? What was the child told and by whom? What was the parent told and by whom? What are the referral and presenting problems? Asking and answering these questions constitutes the beginning of the assessment phase.

During the assessment, the worker has to obtain the biopsychosocial history, including medical, mental health, psychological, and educational data. After the assessment, a treatment plan is developed. Planning involves developing age-appropriate interventions with client and client-related systems. Consideration is also given to the duration of the therapeutic counseling with the child and planning for discharge from the program.

Individual therapeutic counseling sessions occur during the school day. Arrangements must be made with the principal, in order to provide services to a child in accordance with school policies and procedures. For example, can a child be removed from the classroom during an academic subject? Or can he or she attend counseling sessions only during lunch time? At other times, unscheduled walk-in sessions might be held for an immediate concern, such as when a child is having a temper tantrum or is crying uncontrollably for no apparent reason. These sessions usually occur when school personnel experience a child's behavior as unmanageable in the moment.

Group therapeutic counseling sessions should be organized to address issues that interfere with children's academic and social functioning. Groups can be gender-specific or coed. They can be theme-focused or not. They can be time-limited or operate throughout the school year. They can be open or closed groups.

Family sessions can be held either at school, home, or the central office. Whenever possible, accommodations should be made to meet with families during evening hours, if needed. All those living in the household, significant others, and extended family should be allowed to participate, when deemed appropriate.

Crisis intervention is a necessary treatment modality and includes, but is not limited to, assisting with behaviors such as fighting, suspension, suicidal risk, sexual and/or physical abuse allegations, and loss of control. Upon learning of a crisis situation—typically after it has already been managed by school personnel—the mental health worker should immediately contact the school-based mental health supervisor in order to share information, gain feedback, and receive needed emotional support. Sometimes, the mental health worker is brought into a crisis situation while a child is waiting for a parent or an ambulance to arrive.

There are also times when a child reveals information during a therapeutic session that requires the school-based mental health worker to take action—for example, to contact child protective services pursuant to allegations of some form of abuse, or to send the child to the emergency room for an immediate psychiatric evaluation due to plans to commit suicide.

Classroom observations are extremely useful for gathering information about the child's academic functioning and social interactions in the classroom. Observations are made based upon the willingness of the child to be observed by the school-based mental health worker. Classroom observations should be discussed with the teacher (i.e., the goal of the observation, date, and time). All classroom observations should be recorded in the case record.

Home visits should be made, if allowed, whenever there is a need. Some reasons to make a home visit are (a) to meet with a family that cannot keep an appointment at the school, (b) to accommodate a family with a sick or disabled person, and (c) to engage a reluctant family.

During the course of therapeutic counseling, it is essential to obtain copies of school report cards throughout the year. Grades, attendance, academic progress, and teachers' comments provide a record of the student's educational achievements and may validate or invalidate information given by the student and family.

Helpful Hints

- Confirm when therapeutic counseling sessions will be provided.
- Determine the type of intervention to be used.
- Make classroom observations as needed.
- Make home visits, if allowed.
- Obtain copies of school report cards.

Chapter 10

What Does a Mental Health Professional Need to Know About Supervising a School-Based Mental Health Worker?

Supervising a School-Based Mental Health Worker

The supervisor must have the appropriate qualifications and credentials to supervise a mental health worker. To achieve the most effective outcomes, the supervisor should provide a minimum of one hour of weekly uninterrupted individual supervision to the school-based mental health professional. This is in addition to group supervision, if applicable. Supervision is to be in compliance with any state regulations or licensing laws governing the supervision of a mental health professional.

School personnel are *not* to assume supervision of mental health agency staff. Frequently, principals will act as if the mental health worker is a school employee and treat her or him accordingly. This is inappropriate and unacceptable. The mental health program leadership is advised to establish clear boundaries about the supervision of mental health staff so as to avoid confusion and conflicts between the organizations.

Determine where supervision will take place. Will it be at one school setting, to which the supervisor will travel? Will the supervisor go to each school setting so the worker does not have to travel? Does the supervisor provide supervision at the central office?

The advantage of providing school-based supervision is that it affords the supervisor the opportunity to be in the school environment and to get a sense of the lay of the land. The supervisor obtains information firsthand by viewing the environment and, possibly, meeting clients. Also, a school-based supervisor is in the position to respond in a more timely manner to the school-based mental health professional.

The disadvantage to providing school-based supervision is that the supervisor has to be responsible for carrying relevant documents and confidential records back and forth when traveling between locations.

Supervision can be provided at the central office. When supervision is regularly provided at the central office, the supervisor should make time to visit the schools during the course of the year. School visits provide a wealth of information about the aesthetics of the school-based office, the suitability of the space, the supplies and equipment used by staff, and more. A school visit can be a real eye-opener in understanding the daily operations of the school-based mental health program.

Schedule and hold weekly staff meetings. These meetings create bonding, support, and camaraderie among workers who are, typically, separated from one another during the week by virtue of working in different schools.

Conduct or make available regularly scheduled clinical case conferences to discuss referrals, treatment plans, treatment goals and objectives, and treatment progress of students referred to the school-based mental health program. Conduct or make available regularly scheduled administrative meetings to review policies and procedures, to give announcements and updates, to answer questions, to provide feedback, and to share general information.

The supervisor should not be overloaded with too many supervisees. The supervisees should not be overloaded with too many referred children. Remember: your supervisees are working autonomously and are isolated in ways that are uncommon to mental health professionals based in outpatient mental health clinics and hospital settings. Respond as soon as possible to any telephone or electronic outreach made to you by your supervisee.

Helpful Hints

- Determine who will provide supervision, where, when, and how often.
- Ensure that the supervisor has the appropriate qualifications and credentials to supervise the school-based mental health worker.
- Decide whether the supervisor will be situated in the school or central office.
- Schedule and hold weekly uninterrupted individual supervision meetings.
- Schedule and hold weekly staff meetings.
- Conduct regularly scheduled administrative meetings and clinical case conferences.
- Remember: your supervisees are working autonomously and in an isolated manner. Be timely and responsive.

Chapter 11

What Does a Mental Health Professional Need to Know About Supervising Social Work, Psychology, and Mental Health Counseling Interns?

Supervision of Master-Level Students

Graduate students studying to be social workers, psychologists, and mental health counselors are sometimes placed in schools as interns. This is a natural fit because their time in the internship usually coincides with the graduate school academic calendar.

There are competing thoughts about when the intern should inform the child about their length of time in the internship. The authors recommend that the child be informed at the beginning of the therapeutic counseling relationship; the intern should clearly articulate being scheduled to leave the school setting at the end of the school year. The child is entitled to a thoughtful and clinically appropriate beginning and end to the therapeutic relationship, which is best achieved when the intern shares this information at the beginning of the relationship.

It is important for children to experience a farewell in a compassionate manner. This is especially true for children who have experienced sudden loss and/or abandonment. For example, children in foster care who are moved to different homes frequently do not have the opportunity to say good-bye to extended family members, friends, teachers, classmates, neighbors, or even pets. They often leave behind belongings and treasured items when they are moved abruptly from one home to another. One week they are in one school, the next week in a new school. These moves, which may occur several times during a brief period, are abrupt and bewildering, to say the least. The negative effects of these moves are compounded by the lack of a good-bye when needed.

Last but not least, children often hold the erroneous belief that they are somehow responsible for the intern's departure. Maybe if they "weren't bad," the intern would stay.

For all these reasons, school-based mental health interns are encouraged to prepare a child months ahead of time for the inevitable ending of their relationship.

Helpful Hints

- Master-level students are a natural fit for an internship in a public school, given that the graduate-level academic calendar resembles that of the public school.
- These authors recommend children should be informed at the beginning of the therapeutic relationship that the intern will be leaving at the end of the school's academic year.
- Children deserve a respectful and planned end to their relationship with the school-based mental health worker. Prepare a child for the end of the therapeutic relationship, accordingly.

Chapter 12

What Does a Mental Health Professional Need to Know About Staff Turnover?

Staff Turnover

Staff turnover can be high in a school-based mental health program, because there tends to be little room for vertical movement within the organizational hierarchy in such programs. Anecdotally speaking, school-based mental health workers pursue new career opportunities after three to four years.

Unfortunately, after this length of time, school personnel become dependent on the worker. Losing a school-based mental health worker who understands school policies and procedures, has formed valuable collegial relationships, has been integral to the referral process, and knows how to navigate within the school setting leaves a distinct void. Placing a newly hired school-based mental health worker in an already established program is very much like implementing a new school-based mental health program.

It is essential that the mental health agency begin the recruitment process for a new worker as soon as the agency learns there will be a vacant position. Getting the recruitment and hiring process underway as soon as possible minimizes the gap in services left by the departing worker.

If necessary, the program should use a transitional person until a new worker is hired, to provide a measure of continuity in services. This transitional person is often the supervisor. The void can also be filled by one or more of the other mental health workers on the team, if schedules permit. Providing a transitional person closes the gap in services while demonstrating to the school the program's commitment to the students. Continuity of care benefits the child in that the child's progress in treatment is maintained in the best way possible.

Gaps in therapeutic counseling can be a factor in a child's regressive behavior. Children are extremely sensitive to feelings of being abandoned or rejected. They can be prone to acting out sad and angry feelings about the loss of their mental health counselor. They may also think that they were the cause of that person's departure. In addition, communication between the adults is lost when there is a vacancy left by a school-based mental health worker.

A transitional person can continue to support the child and information can continue to be shared among service providers, school, and family. However, the optimal approach would be to have a newly hired school-based mental health worker ready to begin work within a week of a former worker's departure.

Helpful Hints

- Initiate the recruitment process to hire a new school-based mental health worker as soon as a departure is announced.
- In the event of a vacancy, use a transitional person to provide therapeutic counseling services until a new school-based mental health worker is hired.
- Use a transitional person, if necessary, to maintain communication between the service provider, school, and family.

Chapter 13

What Does a Mental Health Professional Need to Know About Summer Activities?

Summer Activities

Provision of therapeutic counseling services during the summer months is particularly challenging due to many factors. Financial support may have to come from different sources. The availability of children as well as the availability of space may fluctuate. It is likely the school-based mental health program will undergo a partial redesign during the summer months. The summer months lend a distinctly different feel to the program, given the absence of school personnel. Not all schools are open during the summer. There may be restriction of space due to school maintenance and repairs. Advance budgeting for the summer program is essential so that adequate supplies will be on hand for summer activities. All of these areas have to be carefully explored prior to planning for summer activities.

Some children and families are unavailable during the summer due to vacation travel, sleep-away camp schedules, visits to out-of-town relatives, or a tendency among some to stay away from the school building during the summer months. Thus, it is important to determine the number of children who will be available during the summer by inquiring of the children and their families at least one month prior to planning summer activities.

These authors have experienced some measure of success during the summer by offering activities that closely resemble a day camp. The school-based mental health supervisor must secure a space in the school large enough to accommodate a group of eight to ten children. Age-appropriate socialization skills plus recreational activities are offered. These activities include outings to nearby parks, zoos, and movie theaters, or bus outings that can be easily financed. The children are fed snacks and/or lunch during the day, depending upon the operating hours. The program can be designed as a half-day or full-day program. All of this depends upon funding, policies, and regulations for the program.

As an alternative, and when appropriate to do so, the school-based mental health worker can assist low-income families in enrolling their children in a day camp or sleep-away camp that offers scholarships, sponsorships, or subsidies.

Helpful Hints

- Plan to undergo a redesign of the school-based mental health program during the summer.
- Decide how summer activities will be paid for and what supplies are needed.
- Determine the number of children who will attend during the summer by inquiring of the children and families at least one month prior to planning summer activities.
- Summer therapeutic counseling activities must be designed within the context of funding, policies, and regulations for the program.
- Assist low-income families, when appropriate, in enrolling their children in a day camp or a sleep-away camp that offers scholarships, sponsorships, or subsidies.

Conclusion

The idea of a school-based mental health program is not new. Although many important guidebooks have been written that emphasize the socioeconomic and political context of on-site school mental health services, the step-by-step process of program planning and implementation appears absent from the literature. These authors chose to address this gap in knowledge based on having experienced the many unique challenges in developing and implementing school-based mental health programs in the New York City public school system. There were a myriad of issues to work through at every level (macro, mezzo, and micro) in order to launch and sustain successful programs despite verbal agreement between the collaborating partners about the stated mission and goals of individual programs.

This book is organized to highlight what mental health professionals need to know from the outset when planning and implementing a school-based mental health program. Specifically, mental health professionals need (a) clarity about mission and goals; (b) clarity about the best way to deliver services, theoretically and philosophically; (c) transparency in communication between mental health professionals and involved parties—school administrators, teachers, staff, parents, at-risk youth, and so on; (d) clarity about the ethical handling of specialized information—that is, from whom, for what purpose, and the potential benefits based on types and levels of administrative and clinical interactions; (e) clarity about fees and payments for services; and (f) last but not least, clarity about who the school liaison responsible for making referrals will be and that individual's commitment to the program. When these essential elements are in place, a successful program is more likely to emerge as a result of the collaborative efforts of all committed partners.

While these authors recognize that there are many ways to measure a program's success, we believe the best measure of success is evidenced when students like Matthew begin to demonstrate increased self-esteem, improved grades, and academic achievement, despite having been impacted by poverty, violence, abuse, and neglect, as are so many youth living in urban areas. Recognition of the therapeutic benefits Matthew and students like him have gained from school-based mental health services and interventions has propelled us to write this guidebook as a means of advocating and offering practical suggestions and helpful hints. We hope and believe this information will lead to the creation of more school-based mental health programs so as to meet the needs of our neediest children.

Appendix I

Orientation and Planning for Collaboration

- Describe mission and goals to be achieved by a school-based mental health program.
- Describe school-based mental health services: individual, group, play, and family therapy; case management; advocacy; home visits; medication therapy; professional trainings to school personnel; and referrals to appropriate outside resources.
- Explain funding sources.
- Explain how the school will benefit by the program—that is, what's in it for the school and students?
- Explain cost to the school.
- Explain cost of services, if any, to families.
- Explain how payment is made. Insurance coverage? Self-pay fees?
- Describe the staffing pattern of the program.
- Provide a schedule of the program's operation hours.
- Give target dates for the beginning and end of the program.

- Describe the roll-out of the program.
- Emphasize the requirement for confidentiality.
- Give details about the goals of school-based meetings to be held with teachers and/or families.
- Explore how the school and program will collaborate to ensure students will receive school-based mental health services in a timely and ongoing manner.
- Under what circumstances will the student *not* be allowed to attend school-based mental health services?
- Determine if the program will be time-limited to the academic year or will be a year-round program. Will the program operate in the summer?
- Determine if the program will be available to all students or to a restricted target population.
- Obtain student population information, including number of students in each grade, language and cultural information, and other relevant statistics and demographic information.
- Describe the type of space needed for the program.
- Explore current availability of space.
- Explore future availability of space, if not available at time of meeting.
- Does availability of space fit in with the time frame for the start-up of the program?
- How are school personnel to be involved in the activities of the school-based mental health program?
- Determine the designated school liaison and contact person for each organization.

- Are those persons in attendance at the orientation meeting? If not, how will introductions be made?
- What other programs will the school-based mental health program interface with (e.g., after-school programs, community-based organizations, and child-serving programs)?
- Will there be an opportunity for collaborative efforts with other programs?
- How will information about the student be shared between the school-based mental health worker and school personnel, in accordance with Health Insurance Portability and Accountability Act (HIPAA), Family Educational Rights and Privacy Act (FERPA) laws, and other governing regulations?
- What happens during a crisis situation? Which rules apply—the school-based mental health program's rules or the department of education (DOE) rules? How do you collaborate on these issues? What will be the understanding?
- What are school policies and procedures? Who is to be involved and what action steps are to be taken? For example, who calls 911 or child protective services? Who makes these decisions? How will the school-based mental health program and school collaborate around these tough decisions?
- What other information will be needed from school personnel (e.g., school calendar, staff professional development days, student exam days, holidays, school closings, etc.)?

- How much access will the school-based mental health program have to academic records beyond school report cards (e.g., cumulative records and attendance records)?
- How late can staff stay in school?
- How will the school-based mental health program be introduced to students and families (i.e., marketing, letters of introductions)?
- Who will be responsible for providing equipment, furnishings, and supplies?
- Describe other services offered by the school-based mental health program (e.g., professional staff development trainings).
- Prior to start-up, school-based mental health staff should look at the proposed office space to be used by the school-based mental health program.
- Identify next steps.

Appendix II

Prepare for Initial Entry into the School

- Determine what supplies and equipment will be needed.
- Ensure that the school-based mental health office is clean and attractive.
- Furnish the office space.
- Display mental health worker's name and hours of operation on office door.
- Make introductions to clerical, administrative, and front-office personnel.
- Give appropriate school personnel relevant school-based mental health contact information.
- Gain possession of keys for the program's office and other areas (e.g., bathroom).
- Obtain educational policies and procedures.
- Obtain schedules for school holidays and professional development days.
- Obtain pupil personnel team (PPT) meeting schedule.
- Obtain student support service team meeting schedule.

- ꞏ Obtain bell schedule showing the time of each class period. This will be a useful tool in planning for meetings with clients, school personnel, and caregivers, and for scheduling inter-agency and intra-agency meetings.
- ꞏ Obtain organizational chart.
- ꞏ Acquire an in-school mailbox for the school-based mental health program.
- ꞏ Learn when report cards are distributed.
- ꞏ Learn when parent-teacher association (PTA) meetings are held.
- ꞏ Determine whether the school or the mental health agency is responsible for Internet access.
- ꞏ Determine who provides for telephone installation other than cell phone service, if applicable.
- ꞏ Determine who will supply in-office equipment.
- ꞏ Determine who will maintain in-office equipment.
- ꞏ Establish a place for filing confidential case records and files.
- ꞏ Determine who will provide maintenance and repair, if needed.
- ꞏ Determine costs, if applicable, to in-school maintenance and repair to the school-based office.
- ꞏ Learn the school policy for delivery of furniture and supplies.
- ꞏ Track the delivery of furniture and supplies, to ensure they are delivered to the school-based mental health program.
- ꞏ Learn the school policy about moving furniture and supplies from one area of the school to another.

- Determine the school policy for minor repairs, painting the office, and decorating. Find out if such work needs formal approvals and/or work orders.
- Determine what school maintenance staff can and cannot do to assist the program.
- Determine what clearances are needed for outside repair persons to do repair work in the school-based mental health program's office.
- Meet and get to know security staff and safety officers.
- Learn fire exits and fire drill procedures.
- Learn the policy about staying after hours in the school building.

Appendix III

Prepare for Annual Reentry into the School

- ○ Ensure that the school-based mental health office is equipped with the appropriate equipment and supplies.
- ○ Place sign on school-based office door showing school-based mental health worker's name, name of program, and hours of operation.
- ○ Give a presentation to the school faculty about the school-based mental health program. This includes differentiating between the roles of the mental health worker, guidance counselor, school psychologist, and other community-based organization staff placed in the school.
- ○ Contact designated school liaison and arrange participation in monthly PPT meetings.
- ○ Develop an agreement with the designated liaison about a protocol for referring children for services within the building.
- ○ Establish a file containing DOE documents such as a policy and procedures manual, chancellor's regulations,

procedures for special education, community resources directory, etc.

- o Obtain bell schedule.
- o Obtain organizational chart.
- o Give appropriate school personnel relevant school-based mental health contact information.
- o Acquire an in-school mailbox for the school-based mental health program.
- o Gain possession of keys for the program's office and other areas (e.g., bathroom).
- o Obtain written criteria for grades and course work.
- o Obtain client referral list from designated school liaison.
- o Obtain classroom schedule for individual children.

Appendix IV

Miscellaneous Things to Consider

- When there is staff turnover in the school, does the new principal/guidance counselor/teacher know about the program?
- Does your designated school liaison continue in her or his role when there are changes within the school's staffing? Are you still receiving referrals? Are you kept informed of meetings? Is there a professional rapport with the new person?
- Interface with school personnel—teachers, security, maintenance, etc.—and key players from other agencies.
- Interface with the PTA.
- Follow school calendar for meetings, half days, holidays, and parent-teacher conferences.
- Accountability: keep school personnel informed about the child—that is, inform them when the child's enrollment status changes, either in the program or in the school.
- Learn the DOE policies and procedures for handling crises.

- Maintain appropriate unshared office space. Do not accept space at the side or back of the auditorium, converted showers and locker rooms, portions of the school library, oversized classrooms, the computer lab, or any space deemed inappropriate for confidential therapeutic counseling sessions. Avoid using the nurse's office.
- Case records are designed to reflect standards and criteria governing work with individual clients. It is necessary for the program to adopt forms that will capture required information for regulatory bodies who govern and provide oversight for school-based mental health services.
- Be prepared for staff turnover, vacant positions, and hiring replacement school-based mental health workers.
- Be prepared to lose the school-based mental health program office, to be used for another purpose within the school. How will you work toward getting a replacement office?
- Be prepared for the theft of school-based mental health program supplies.
- Be prepared for new school administrative staff. Plan to give them an orientation about the school-based mental health program.
- Consider the possibility of competition with other school-based counseling programs, especially those offering free services.
- Obtain school report cards, with written consent, to track academic progress.

References

Cantor, P. A. (2010, August). *Innovative designs for persistently low performing schools: Transforming failing schools by addressing poverty-related barriers to teaching and learning.* Paper presented at the meeting of the Aspen Institute Congressional Education Program, Aspen, CO.

Cusick, G. R., Goerge, R. M., & Bell, K. C. (2009). *From corrections to community: The juvenile re-entry experience as characterized by multiple systems involvement.* Chicago, IL: University of Chicago. Retrieved from https://www.chapinhall.org/sites/default/files/Corrections%20to%20Community_04_21_09.pdf

Dworsky, A. (2008). *Educating homeless children in Chicago: A case study of children in the family regeneration program.* Chicago, IL: University of Chicago. Retrieved from https://www.chapinhall.org/sites/default/files/ChapinHallDocument(2).pdf

Goren, S. G. (1996). The wonderland of social work in schools. In R. Constable, J. P. Flynn & S. McDonald (Eds.), *School social work: Practice and research perspectives* (3rd ed., pp. 57–65). Chicago, IL: Lyceum Books.

Greene, R. R., & Frankel, K. (1994). A systems approach: Addressing diverse family forms. In R. R. Greene (Ed.), *Human behavior theory: A diversity framework* (pp. 147–171). Hawthorne, NY: Aldine de Gruyter.

Kominski, R., Jamieson, A., & Martinez, G. (2001). At-risk conditions of U.S. school-age children. *Working Paper Series, No. 52.* Washington, DC: Population Division U.S. Bureau of the Census. Retrieved from https://www.census.gov/population/www/documentation/twps0052/twps0052.html#abs

Lewis, J. S., & Greene, R. R. (1994). Working with natural social networks: An ecological approach. In R. R. Greene (Ed.), *Human behavior theory: A diversity framework* (pp. 203–216). Hawthorne, NY: Aldine de Gruyter.

Mayer, S. (2005). *Educating Chicago's court-involved youth: Mission and policy in conflict.* Chicago, IL: University of Chicago. Retrieved from http://www.chapinhall.org/sites/default/files/old_reports/209.pdf

Smithgall, C., Gladden, R. W., Yang, D., & Goerge, R. (2005). *Behavior problems and educational disruptions among children in out-of-home care in Chicago.* Chapin Hall Working Paper. Chicago, IL: University of Chicago. Retrieved from https://www.chapinhall.org/sites/default/files/old_reports/256.pdf

TRUE DIRECTIONS

An affiliate of Tarcher Perigee

OUR MISSION

Tarcher Perigee's mission has always been to publish books that contain great ideas. Why? Because:

GREAT LIVES BEGIN WITH GREAT IDEAS

At Tarcher Perigee, we recognize that many talented authors, speakers, educators, and thought-leaders share this mission and deserve to be published – many more than Tarcher Perigee can reasonably publish ourselves. True Directions is ideal for authors and books that increase awareness, raise consciousness, and inspire others to live their ideals and passions.

Like Tarcher Perigee, True Directions books are designed to do three things: inspire, inform, and motivate.

Thus, True Directions is an ideal way for these important voices to bring their messages of hope, healing, and help to the world.

Every book published by True Directions– whether it is non-fiction, memoir, novel, poetry or children's book – continues Tarcher Perigee's mission to publish works that bring positive change in the world. We invite you to join our mission.

For more information, see the True Directions website:

www.iUniverse.com/TrueDirections/SignUp

Be a part of Tarcher Perigee's community to bring positive change in this world! See exclusive author videos, discover new and exciting books, learn about upcoming events, connect with author blogs and websites, and more!
www.tarcherbooks.com

TRUE DIRECTIONS

AN AFFILIATE OF TARCHER PERIGEE

Printed in the United States
By Bookmasters